# DOT TO DOT ZEN

*A Primer of Buddhist Psychology*

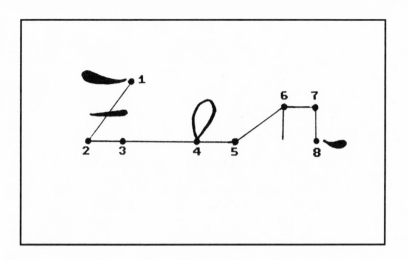

# DOT TO DOT ZEN

*A Primer of Buddhist Psychology*

Gerald L. Ericksen

Charles E. Tuttle Company, Inc.
Boston • Rutland, Vermont • Tokyo

Published in the United States in 1993 by
Charles E. Tuttle Company, Inc. of Rutland, Vermont & Tokyo, Japan,
with editorial offices at 77 Central Street, Boston, Massachusetts 02109.

**Library of Congress Cataloging-in-Publication Data**

Ericksen, Gerald L., 1931-
  Dot to dot Zen : a primer of Buddhist psychology / Gerald L.
  Ericksen.
    p.  cm.
  Includes bibliographical references.
  ISBN 0-8048-1801-0
  1. Buddhism—Psychology.  I. Title
BQ4570.P76E75  1993
294.3'422—dc20                                              92-5665
                                                              CIP

Cover design by Mary Ericksen

PRINTED IN THE UNITED STATES ON ACID-FREE PAPER

# ACKNOWLEDGMENTS

Connected moments of insight are gratefully acknowledged: *forms* of expression from Linda Smith, quiet *feelings* from Godwin Samaratna's Meditation Center, new *perceptions* from John Holt's Fulbright program, supportive *volition* from my family, and a heightened *consciousness* of Zen from Padmasiri de Silva.

# PREFACE

The following pages may be viewed as a small mirror, reflecting ancient Asian concepts of mind and body. Repeated three part segments are interwoven in the spirit of Buddhist psychology which is, simultaneously, an act of direct experience and a perception of the act: both doer and observer; both the understanding mind and the mind understood.

Visual koans in the form of dot-to-dots, together with brief excerpts or reflections of classical Oriental aphorisms and metaphors which the images represent; a brief interpretation of the teachings; and an integrated sequence of practical meditational thoughts are the repetitive forms selected for this interaction of hand, eye and mind.

Each set represents a step on an ordered path, leading from confusion to a centering of the self.

# CONTENTS

# THE DEVIL OF CONFUSION

— *The Path*, Dhammapada

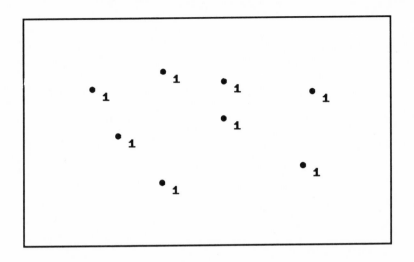

*One beginning, many forms*

Our path begins with a realization that suffering arises from confusion. The nature of this confusion is not knowing where to begin to understand the reality of our self.

**Focus on the breath passing through your nose. . .**

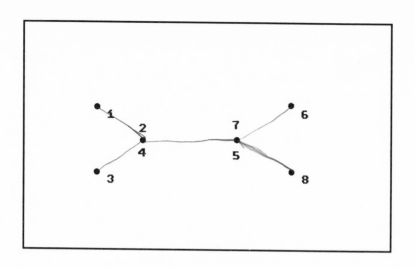

*Time flees, going nowhere*

What is the boundary between then and now? If now touches the future, is it before? If time flees everywhere, to where does it return? If forms are one at their center, are centers everything? From endless speculations about time and space, shifting uncertainties arise in our mind. Such speculations do not lie on our path of direct experience that leads away from mental anguish.

**Don't force breathing, just focus on it. . .**

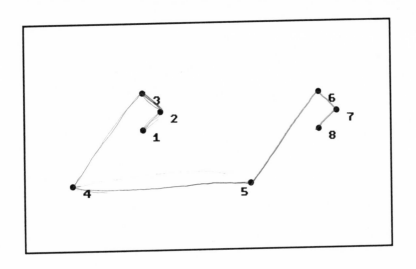

*To know reality is to know that all beings
are bent with suffering*

The degree to which we are bent with suffering changes
with the observer.  Our task is to let go of old perspectives
and to let fall away enslaving attachments with prescribed
beginnings and endings.  Our own thoughts are what make
us suffer for our weaknesses.  By understanding our
thoughts and our weaknesses, we can learn from them.  In
this way, enemies become teachers.

**If your mind wanders, bring it back to breathing. . .**

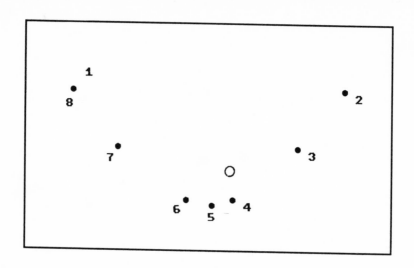

*Clear pools of water, deep thought*

Meditation, as a technique, is a clearing of our vision to see reality as it presents itself, from unifying moment to unifying moment. In this way, specks of imperfection in perceptions of our self, as well as of others, tend to dissolve in a flow of choiceless awareness, undistorted by our own emotions.

**If there is outside noise, note it, and return to breathing. . .**

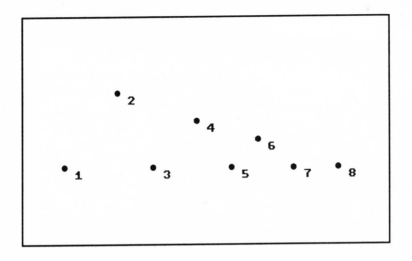

*Lulled, the waves sink*

Meditation, as a technique, is a calming and centering of our complex mind. We attempt to focus our mind in order to experience an ever changing reality.

**Just breathe. . .**

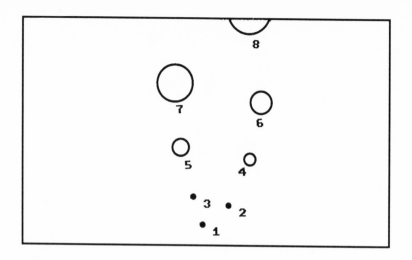

*Look upon the world as you would a bubble*

The experienced reality of breathing is taken as a first line of attack on the suffering of the mind, for, without breath, the mind cannot work; feelings, perceptions, emotions and ideas vanish. Resting upon such an insubstantial, impermanent reality as breath, the seemingly complex mind bares its hollow core.

**If thoughts arise, let them arise and fall away. . .
If sensations arise, let them arise and fall away. . .**

THE MIND IS FICKLE AND FLIGHTY
AND IT FLEES AFTER FANCIES
WHEREVER IT LIKES

— *The Mind*, Dhammapada

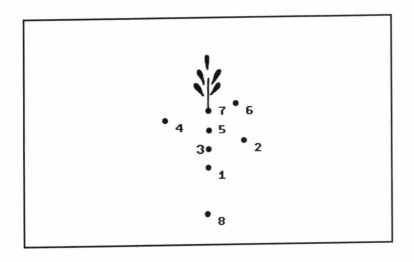

*The farmer mind bustles among its 55 laborers to bring in the sensory harvest*

The senses of eye, ear, nose, tongue and touch never vote with the mind on the issue of attachment. Each goes its own way, seeking its own ends. An old proverb relates how, if bound together by ropes with a common knot, the crocodile tries to run to water, the dog to a village, the fox to a cemetery, the monkey to a forest, and the snake to an anthill, while the bird tries to fly into the sky. The ultimate goal of this path is a vanishing, a complete disappearance of anguish brought on by the baffling array of sense attachments. In this way, the goal is no goal.

**Reducing thoughts makes intervals between thoughts. . .**

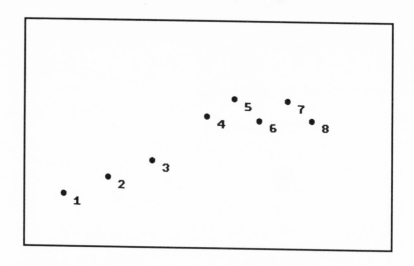

*Swans leave their lake and rise into the air*

Guilt driven suffering is viewed as a thought from the past, no more substantial than any other mental component or sense impression. The changing components of our mind do not belong to any permanent self and certainly not to anyone else. Thus, we can free our mind from pain brought on by others. By flying, the swan becomes swan-like; and, by watching, the changing mind is freed.

**Use your intervals to concentrate on breathing. . .**

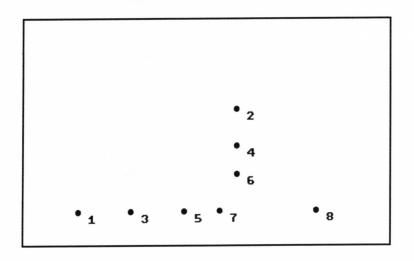

*The wind blows out a fleeting flame*

By observing thoughts from aside, by watching sensations arise and fall away, an awareness is raised about where the mind begins and sensations end. We need not concern ourselves with where thoughts of greed, hatred and delusion flee, or where sickness hides when health flows.

**Focus on the present. . .**

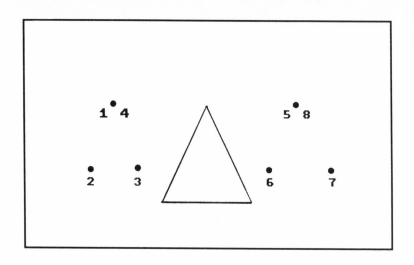

*A tranquil mind looks at both sides equally*

A sudden release from guilt's stranglehold grants temporary probation to a troubled mind; a mind momentarily able to see imprisoned conditions for what they really are. Without a judge's sentence, we can become free by chaining ourselves to the effort of building a road away from categories of right and wrong. We pick our way upward, toward a liberated world in which our observing self is mindful of no distinctions. Nothingness can cut the motivational roots beneath clever speech, aggressive action and cunning livelihoods.

**Try not to let past and future thoughts take over. . .**

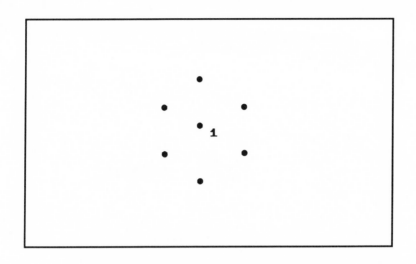

*Defined, then confused, they are the same*

Where, then, does one begin to use the mind to cure the mind of its suffering? The ancient wisdom offered is a path away from the pain of greed, hatred and delusion born of ignorance. This path is comprised, not of conceptual speculation regarding time, space, life's origin or eternal existence, but of realities such as breathing and suffering that we all experience directly. Intuitive knowledge of this experienced reality is available to everyone willing to step back and observe themselves. Experiencing, and knowing that we experience, helps us to rise above a confusion of definitions, to understand what is defined in life if we are not confused.

**Feel the cool air in, the warm air out. . .**

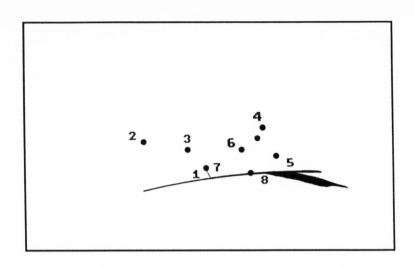

*The alighting bird, at the same moment,*
*strikes the bough and casts a shadow*

We sometimes think, speak and act out of a lack of awareness, inattention or insensitivity; that is, out of ignorance.
These actions weave a chain made from links of sensations,
feelings, cravings and clingings. We bring suffering upon
our self as the impermanent chain slips from our grasp.
The mind, however, need not vibrate with each knock at
sensation's door.

**Put your self in the present. . .**

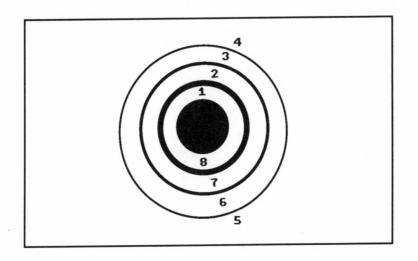

*Tides of universal reversion flow endlessly*

The self, sitting poised in pure emptiness, easily flows outward to a clear vision of truth; out to close encounters with faithful calls to come or to go; resting, finally, with pools of doubt filled with spontaneous and authentic relationships. Dropping off, the egotistic mind and body are lost in a sea beyond self's protective reef. Paradoxically, tides of consciousness move back in toward our original void; mind and body, encrusted with material bonds, activities, judgements and reflections, dropped off in the center of nothingness.

**Let ideas and sensations float by. . .**

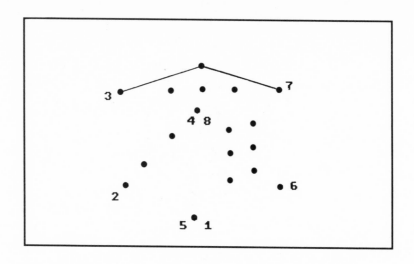

*In the teeming soil, previous seeds await their chance*

From the arising of one link in the chain, the next link arises and, if one link does not arise, the next will also not arise. This path is a training of the mind to bring the connecting links under our control. Being in control, we need not gamble on destructive cravings.

**Let your mind have choiceless awareness. . .**

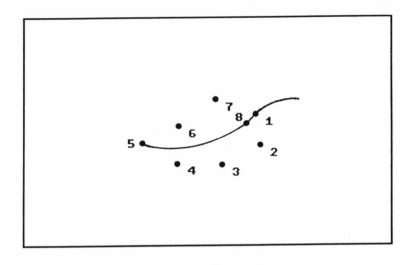

*A single leaf falls, fall is everywhere*

The ability to control our mind makes us masters of our fate. A razor's edge can be held between unalterable sequences of connected arisings in our mind and actions launching the chain of events. In this way, the nature of the outside world can be understood by looking at the world within us.

**Let any thoughts come and disappear,
watching them from aside. . .**

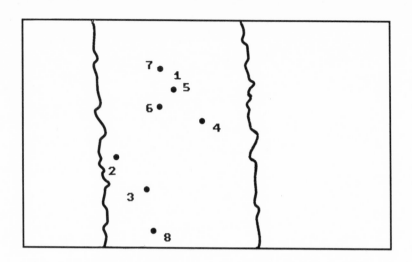

*A raft crossing a strong current, may turn the latter aside for only a moment*

Mental life is a process of passing phenomena. Feelings, perceptions, emotions and memories float endlessly by on life's edge. As change comes, the suffering self tends to grasp for comforting but illusionary stability. This path is an acceptance of the swift current of passing individual sensations and an understanding of the still basin at the end of each.

**Permit unconscious to be conscious. . .**

# CUT DOWN THE FOREST OF DESIRES, NOT ONLY A TREE

— *The Path*, Dhammapada

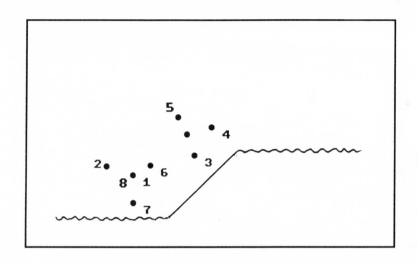

*Against the current of passion. . . bound for joy*

Suffering has intellectual roots arising from delusion about who we are. However, new knowledge does not have to be something we don't already know. Insight meditation is aimed at removing the dam of neutral feelings which form pools of ignorance and delusion. The truth to be unveiled is that mental life is impermanent, lacks lasting substance and is the seedbed of dissatisfaction.

**Remove judgment of our own thought, also of others. . .**

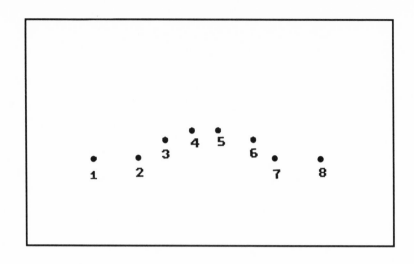

*Something which looks swollen from the outside
is hollow from inside*

Suffering has emotional roots arising from greed. Greed appears both as a leashing to excessive sensory gratification and as an unrealistic emphasis on self-preservation. We seek to preserve our self to perpetuate transient pleasurable feelings about perceptions, emotions, memories and the physical form comprising the self. This path teaches that we are not free, even if we carry our own leash.

**Let thoughts pass by without expectation,
without specific goal. . .**

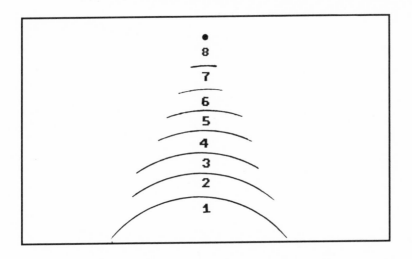

*Clouds retreat, the mountain bones are bared*

Wedging aside worldly desires, momentary concentration expands consciousness to the indifferent clarity of true knowledge. Infinite phenomena pouring in to fill our enlarged vision opens a window to the emptiness beyond. With our mind feeding only on sparse blades of desire and fleeting dreams, we can reach the bare peak of mind's temple, and then leave even it behind.

**Careful talking, careful reading, careful listening gives space between ideas. . .**

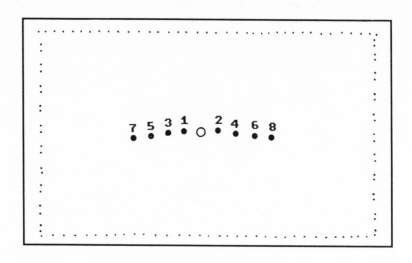

*Right and wrong, blinding tears*

Suffering has emotional roots arising from hatred. Hatred appears both as aggression toward others and as a striving for self-annihilation. Taking excessive notice of others and ourselves we seek to compare ourselves to standards beyond our reach. Aggression is an attempt to remove an unfavorable standard from our self. Self-annihilation is an attempt to remove our self from the painful comparison. This path teaches that hatred will vanish if we are no longer blind to its roots.

**Use the space to return to breathing. . .**

*A raindrop slips into the shining sea*

Tranquillity mediation is aimed at becoming more aware of pleasant feelings that open gates to greed and unpleasant feelings that open gates to hatred. Greed and hatred both race in vain; one toward and the other away from an insubstantial self. Suffering drops away in a calm and extremely alert mind.

**Be mindful of mental chatter...**
**Let thoughts come and pass away...**

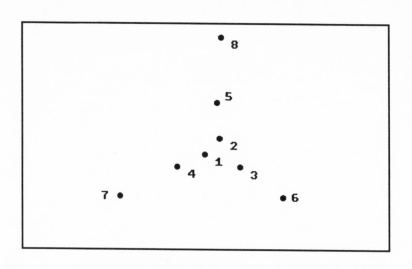

*Swollen by attachments, hollowness grows*

This path starts with our direct experience of the world and frees the mind from the overpowering diversity of reality by analyzing the elements of our perception. In this way, the world is no longer seen as perfectly harmonized and just; nor is it seen as totally hostile and evil. Perceptions, reduced to their fundamental form, let us see that high and low, good and bad, beautiful and ugly are intertwined as part of the same sensory dance.

**Don't fight sensations. . .**
**Be kind to your body, gentle to your mind. . .**

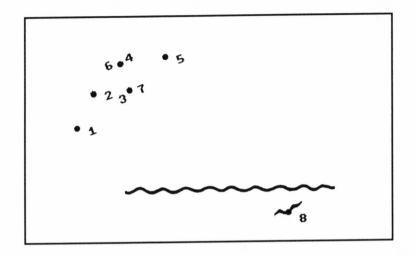

*A gull watches its small shadow in the sea*

Our view of reality affects the pain we can endure. Suffering will arrive in our life; there is no way to prevent illness, aging and death. We can, however, position ourselves in such a way that while pain may be present, our mind is elsewhere. We are not condemned to let involuntary emotions rob us of a wholesome existence.

**A still mind from a still body. . .**

THIS PATH TRAVELS
TO THE END OF SORROW

— *The Path*, Dhammapada

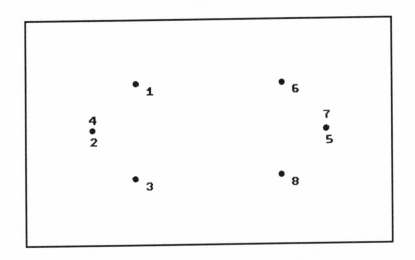

*Two paths: following the heart and leading the mind*

This path is not idle speculation about our anguish. It is not only a basis for action, it is the action itself. It is a realization that to live is to suffer, that the cause of suffering is desire; and that if desire does not arise, neither will suffering. We, ourselves, become the path, leading away from suffering.

**Still thoughts let us be more aware,
and more alert to all about us. . .**

33

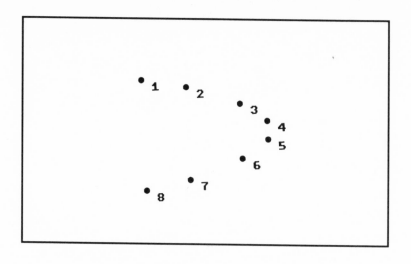

*Finding the path, we can turn ourselves around*

Our existence is fleeting, not under our control and not altogether satisfactory since we do not always know which way we were headed before realizing we were lost. Since subtle actions can have unknown gross consequences we are to be careful in thought, speech and livelihood.

**Now form a subject-object dichotomy...**
**the subject is my consciousness, the object a fear I have...**

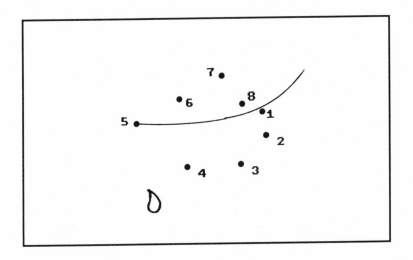

*A drop of water falls from a leaf*

Once released from self-attachments, we need do nothing extra to seek perfection. Unhindered by illusory clinging, we can let go of catchments in which terror may arise. The mind filled with longings, restlessness and trifles has much to fear; but breaking free, it can follow its true nature to perfection. What need one fear when the transient self, itself, is not feared? Just as good cloth easily takes the dye, the mind, being pure at inception, will, if left to fall freely, seek its original level.

**Realize you have automatically transcended
the dichotomy...**

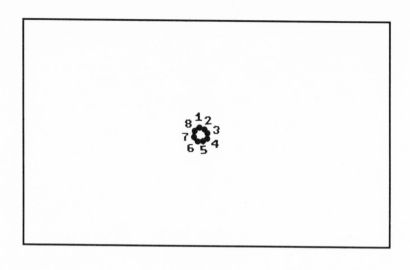

*No gain work*

It is not easy to break free. Ill-will, sensory cravings, laziness, restlessness and remorse, all closely connected, hide the path to peace. Having understood our mind, the search is already completed before we begin a hunt for tranquillity.

**I am the fear. . .**

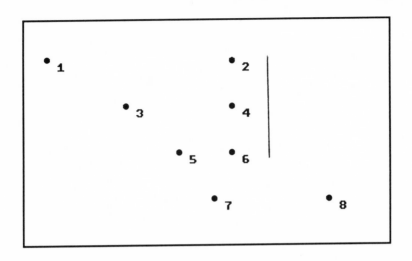

*Yield and overcome*

This path is a busy roadway of doing and undoing. We are to abandon unwholesomeness and perfect our senses. We are to both approach wholesomeness and retreat from evil; to be mindful of each moment's action. After perfection, we need do nothing extra.

**Have the mind quiet and clear,
as a still pool of clear water...**

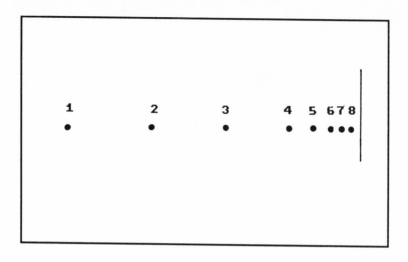

*The mind is capable of infinite extension, but has a limited object of thought*

Progress on this path becomes increasingly difficult for those not under their own control or blinded by delusion. It requires concentration to calm the mind and to experience a choiceless awareness of things just as they are; to attend to just the seen and just the heard with bare attention undistorted by praise, blame, happiness or pain.

**Even a small speck of dirt may be seen in a clear pool. . .**

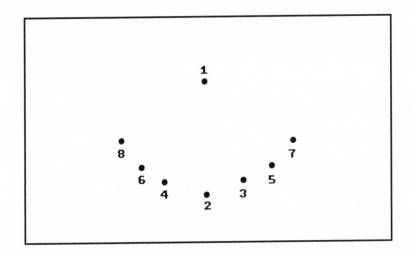

*The falling of drops of water will, in time, fill a bowl*

On this path, our mind is as a bowl. This bowl gradually fills with anguish interwoven with unwholesomeness, but when emptied, it reveals a pattern of wholesome joy. Cleansing our mind, however, is not done quickly, but rather with subtle insights and small actions of restraint and loving kindness.

**Even a small signal of fear or anger may be observed with a still mind...**

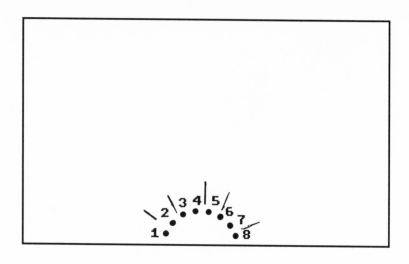

*As does the sun, wisdom rises gently*

Looking back, with firm conviction, at weakened pride and a loosened hold of superstition, we begin to find our enlightened mind. We have already shed light on the path which crosses the stream of delusion. Driven back, we can try once more with a load lightened by less hatred and less clinging to our senses. Looking back, finally, from across the far bank, we can recognize the dark flotsam of restlessness, conceit and abstractions of our mind drifting far downstream.

**By observing the small signal it tends to dissolve. . .**

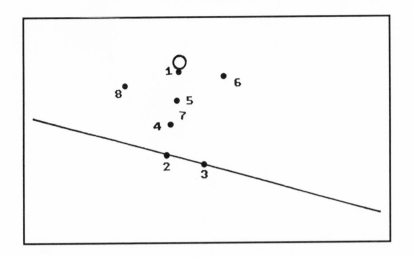

*Balance is the absence of wavering*

We are constantly reminded, by our own breath, to be mindful of the stones on the path. Balance and concentration are needed for each step; since, being swayed by greed, hatred and delusion, our vision becomes misted; filled with impermanence, lack of substance and dissatisfaction.

**Return to breathing...**

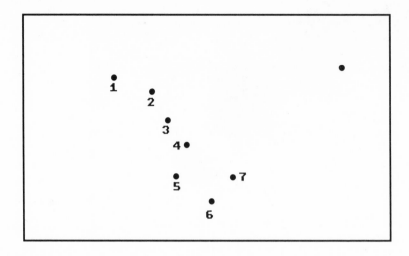

*Who can trace the path of those who soar in the sky of liberation?*

Weightless Ursa Major, tethered to its bright Polaris, circles endlessly, leaving no trace on its unnumbered path. In the same way, a clean cut through our appointed task leaves no trace of others, separating us from clinging hatred. Quickly setting our finished effort aside, we carry no trace of our self, freed from clinging pride. Without error, the big dipper fills and empties itself as it continues on its appointed rounds; without ignorance, we carefully pass through our work.

**The goal is to dissolve the ego...**

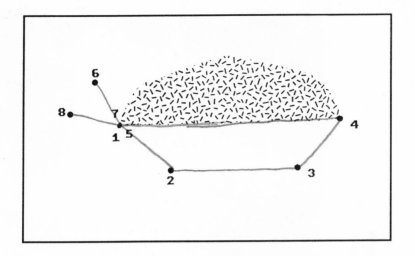

*When your rice-pot is full to the brim,*
*one can only take niggling bits*

Defilements in our mind are fallen trees and impure water on this path. Colored waters of sensory craving, boiling water of ill-will, windblown water of restlessness, moss-grown water of laziness and the dark water of remorse all are hindrances to reflecting on ourselves as we truly are.

**Do nothing, return to breathing. . .**

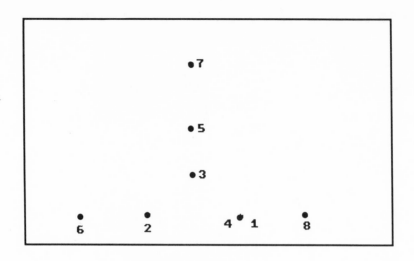

*From subtle thought, grand actions arise*

Neutral feelings lead to forms of delusion, unpleasant feelings arouse forms of ill-will, and pleasant feelings arouse forms of greed. In turn, delusion gives rise to denial, ill-will to anger, and greed to bargaining. Exposed denial, spent anger and failed bargains give rise to the depression of realizing that, once done, even the smallest actions can not be undone by the purest of thoughts.

**Accept us for what we all are. . .**
**No need to distort ourselves. . .**

# THIS BODY IS THE FOAM OF A WAVE

— *The Flowers of Life*, Dhammapada

*Not very far goes the perfume of flowers*

Transient happiness is not peace. The fruits of greed soon spoil. Senses, always groping anew, are never gratified for long; and to be slave to them is to be consumed by futile hope for preservation of a mortal self.

**With a clear mind we may be hurt,
but we can accept it as reality. . .**

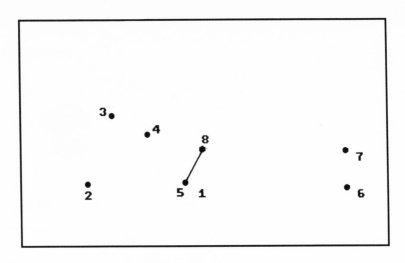

*A tree, though cut down, can grow again*
*if its roots are undamaged*

This path is not a shortcut to happiness. It is a journey to peace, away from evil growing from old seed. Aggression and self-destruction are quick, violent attempts to temporarily remove the pain caused by clinging to a false self.

**A detached mind sees reality**
**undistorted by language and concepts. . .**

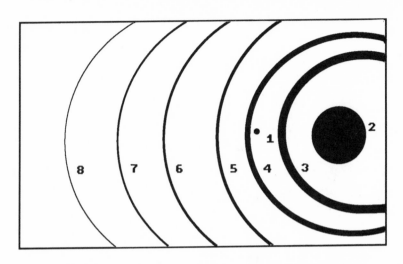

*As the bell is simply struck, the gateway to reality is open.*

Distortions and impurities, appearing to originate beyond us, may be but corruptions of the mind. Awakened and attentive, even before the note is struck, we can turn the barely audible into clarion calls of true fundamental notes playing all about us. Distorting pure sounds and attending to impure overtones are as two fools; one failing to discharge their own duties and the other undertaking duties which are properly of someone else. The fundamental hum notes of existence become distorted by our own failed judgements based on ill-will, dullness, fear or a falsely claimed authority.

**A detached mind sees reality undistorted by emotions. . .**

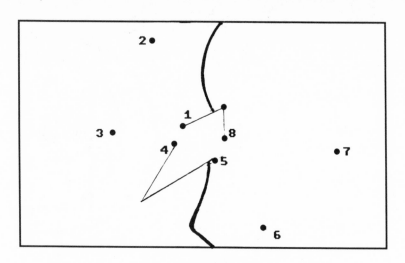

*The butterfly sleeps well, perched on the temple bell . . .*
*until it rings*

Vibrating bells, gongs, and drums are but calls to wake up to a new strength, yielding and powerful; to leave behind ill-will, craving, torpor, restlessness and doubt; to understand our mind as being impermanent, insubstantial and our source of anguish. They are calls to beat greed into compassion, hatred into kindness and delusion into insight.

**No need to search for creativity. . .**

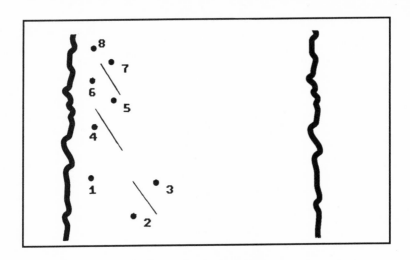

*One river, many rafts*

By not clinging to feelings we better understand our reality. Peaceful acceptance lies on three well-traveled branches of the same path: compassion and fellowship of others seeking the way, beckoning calls of a compassionate faith, and the charge to go alone by controlling your own mind.

**Creativity comes from a calm mind. . .**

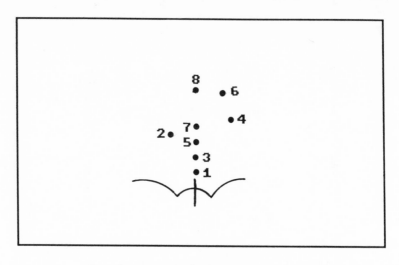

*A seed sprouts in the field through causes*

Having interconnected causes, each perplexing thought drives another. The good done by virtue is temporary and concentration's quiet focus gives way, again, to life's influx. Through an intuitive understanding, an introspective experiencing of the mind, we can nourish these moments of peaceful reflection.

**Know the four blocks to meditation. . .**
**Intellectualizing. . .**
**Strong positive feelings about self. . .**
**Strong negative feelings about self. . .**
**Laziness. . .**

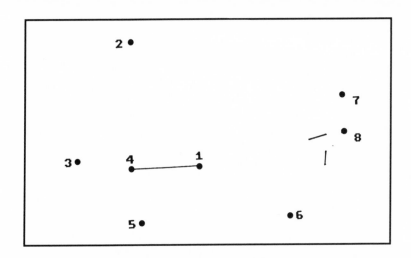

*From the pine tree learn of the pine tree,
and from bamboo of the bamboo*

Lost and frozen with fear, we stand alone in a forest of hindrances; unwilling to proceed intellectually, unable to retreat emotionally and terrified to remain in our present void. We are taught that, at this precise location, we find our true self, without moving, already standing in the Zen clearing of our mind. It is an opening from which we can authentically experience a brief view, beyond impermanent barriers of our vision, to a reality lying deep within us. To understand the nature of individual trees is to change our view of the forest. The peaceful way out is an enlightened path, carved out by a readiness to confront our own mind.

**Overcome the blocks to meditation. . .**

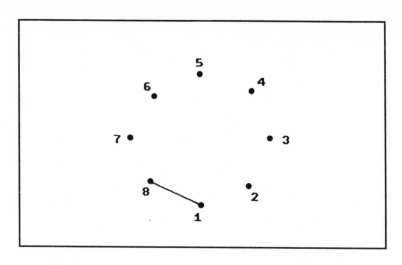

*The cow and the man both gone out of sight*

The confusion of a mind on fire may be cleared away by concentrated attention on impermanence and the linked consequences of our actions. Both the boundaries of the mind and the phenomena it views quickly shift. Knowledge of the shifting nature of our existence justifies our waiting with clenched teeth for feelings, heavy with craving, to fall under their own weight. Serene loving-kindness can overcome aggressive weeds of hate and, by turning away, we shake off entangled creepers of past wrongdoing. Thoughtful inaction leaves us momentarily free of worldly dualism, quickly poised for new and wholesome fresh action. Thus our endless deaths come and go.

**No need to know how to react to others,
it will be spontaneous to the moment...**

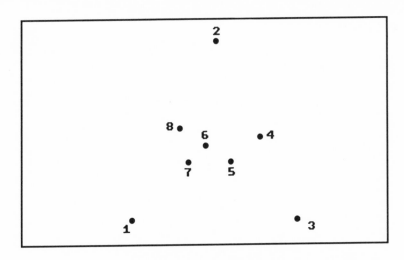

*On high, the winds blow cool*

At any moment, it rests within our power to cool the consuming flame of craving; to raise ourselves up to a release from the oppressive wheel of suffering returning again and again in our lifetime.

**Return to breathing...**

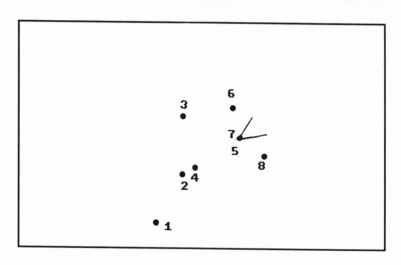

*The simple blossoms are windblown*

At any moment, many things influence us: our presence together, a light breeze in a window, a sunbeam on the floor, and on and on to thousands of things. Changing any single element can change the dependent origination of the moment.

**View guilt as a thought passing from the past. . .**

COME AND LOOK AT THIS WORLD!
IT IS LIKE A ROYAL PAINTED CHARIOT
WHEREIN FOOLS ARE IMPRISONED

—*Arise and Watch*, Dhammapada

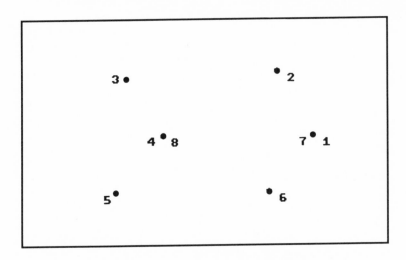

*Real actions, illusionary actions*

Our mind comprehends only outlines and shadows of all about us and yet takes this to be a permanent reality, absorbing all of the problems and stress of this apparent reality. Our attempt is to separate our consciousness from this mind-set to get inside and below the outlines of reality.

**Have no expectations of yourself or others. . .**

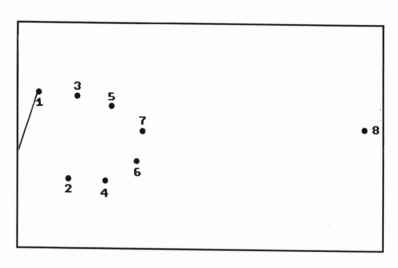

*All things, indeed, pass away*

We, each through our own lenses, observe a changing, impermanent world. The five senses dance for the mind under craving's direction. Excessive personal involvement can be a haze over our mind; for, what is wrongly perceived, is wrongly conceived. A self swollen with desire is a lense thickened with impurity.

**Try not to retreat, but rather to be alert. . .**

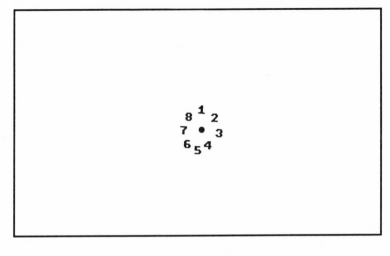

*One thing, many names*

Things take on different labels because of our senses. To see the world accurately, we need to make peace with our perceptions by letting sensations be simply sensations, as the world is just the world. Superiority, inferiority and equality are all but forms of conceit, requiring advertisement of self. In the same way, self-pity is merely a near enemy of compassion, as is indifference of patience, restraint of hatred and greed of love.

**Egotism says, 'I did it, I was totally responsible.'**

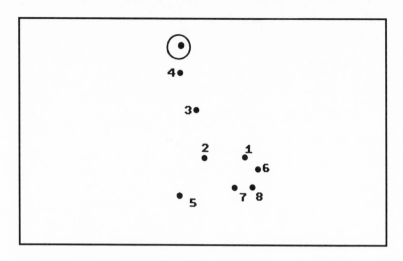

*Sitting in meditation, the mind is free to vanish*

In meditation we become above our self, observing our self participating in the dependent realities of the moment. This separation of ego and consciousness provides a distance, whereby consuming emotions, attached to the psychological dependency of the moment, are reduced.

**Sit and watch your emotions work. . .**

| A | 04 | 19 | 32 | 43 | 55 | 14 |
| B | 25 | 33 | 43 | 49 | 64 | 04 |
| C | 42 | 46 | 51 | 54 | 57 | 07 |
| D | 01 | 23 | 37 | 48 | 63 | 15 |
| E | 01 | 05 | 07 | 34 | 70 | 07 |

## TUE JAN17 17
## $5.00

02296800 337-038564145-126729 013159
SAT JAN14 17 20:11:03

EVERY DAY IN JANUARY BUY
$5 OF PLAY PACK AND
RECEIVE A $2 CASH4LIFE
QUICK PICK FREE
(UP TO $20 PURCHASE)

## IMPORTANT INFORMATION

This ticket is a bearer instrument. You must be 18 years or older to purchase a New York Lottery ticket. A prize up to and including $600 may be claimed and paid at any NY Lottery Retailer within 1 year of the drawing. A Bonus Free Play must be claimed at a Retailer within 1 year of the drawing. You may claim any cash prize at a Lottery Customer Service Center (see nylottery.ny.gov for locations), or complete this ticket by filling in the form below and mailing to:

New York Lottery, P.O. Box 7533, Schenectady, NY 12301-7533

All cash prizes must be claimed within one year of the drawing. All tickets, transactions and winners are subject to New York State Laws and New York Lottery Rules and Regulations.

NAME (PLEASE PRINT LEGIBLY)

STREET

CITY     STATE     ZIP CODE

EMAIL ADDRESS     PHONE NUMBER

SIGNATURE     SOCIAL SECURITY NUMBER

NY-1003-01   Rev. 1/16

**NEW YORK** STATE OF OPPORTUNITY | **Gaming Commission**

**GAMBLING PROBLEM?**
24-Hour Confidential Hopeline
Call 877-8-HOPENY
or text HOPENY (467369)
NOT A RESULTS LINE

Hey, you never know.

NYLOTTERY.NY.GOV

**Please Play Responsibly.**
You must be at least 18 years of age to purchase a lottery ticket.

YA 0882525306

## IMPORTANT INFORMATION

This ticket is a bearer instrument. You must be 18 years or older to purchase a New York Lottery ticket. A prize up to and including $600 may be claimed and paid at any NY Lottery Retailer within 1 year of the drawing. A Bonus Free Play must be claimed at a Retailer within 1 year of the drawing. You may claim any cash prize at a Lottery Customer Service Center (see nylottery.ny.gov for locations), or complete this ticket by filling in the form below and mailing to:

New York Lottery, P.O. Box 7533, Schenectady, NY 12301-7533

All cash prizes must be claimed within one year of the drawing. All tickets, transactions and winners are subject to New York State Laws and New York Lottery Rules and Regulations.

NAME (PLEASE PRINT LEGIBLY)

STREET

CITY     STATE     ZIP CODE

EMAIL ADDRESS     PHONE NUMBER

SIGNATURE     SOCIAL SECURITY NUMBER

NY-1003-01   Rev. 1/16

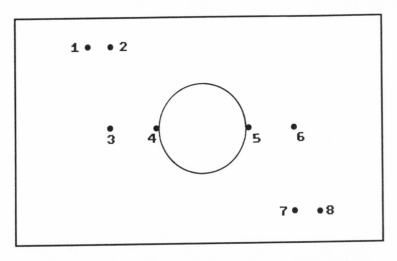

*Superiority and inferiority equally pedal the same empty ego*

Mind's road to freedom is an endless turning of comparisons back on itself. In gradual stages, foothills of sensual pleasures and harmful states of consciousness fall beneath us on our downstrokes; while goodwill, pity, empathy and equanimity rise on our upstroke. Cresting, the apparent peaks of material gain, sense reactions and perceived differences give way to a plane of infinite space and consciousness, a nothingness.

**Sit and watch your intellect work. . .**

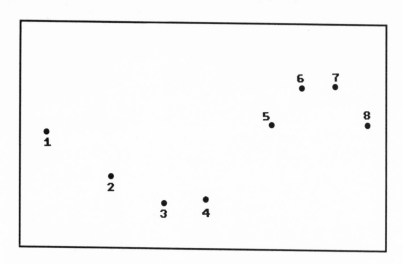

*True knowledge is neither happy nor sad, neither long nor short*

In meditation, we quickly become aware of our states of mind for we can not be happy or sad for long without knowing it. However we also recognize the ephemeral nature of these emotions.

**No need to act serious and sad. . .**

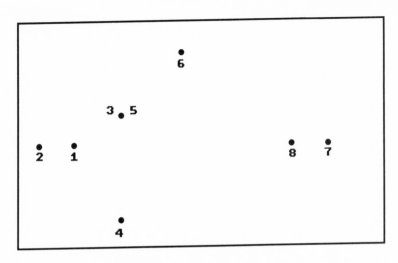

*Rain breaks through an ill-thatched roof*

Virtue repairs the sensory flaws through which suffering
enters. Whether suddenly, or slowly and indirectly, we
bring upon ourselves the consequences of our own
thoughts and deeds. Virtue simplifies a tangled life, allows
reflective control of our own mind and permits the tranquillity to enjoy wisdom's beauty. Semblances of ethics, philosophy and religion all follow this single-minded effort to
shed suffering.

**With a calm mind, we can confront ourselves. . .**

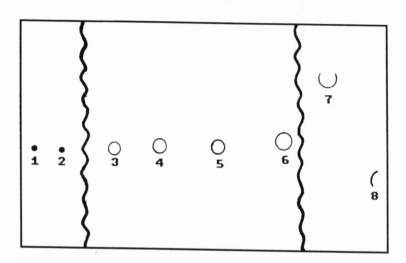

*Subtle and hard to see, freedom's path is empty, signless, aimless*

A mind brought under self control is free to roam, unhindered, beyond its own narrow boundaries. Clever knots binding others to us are but self deceptions regarding the true nature of a relationship. A mind reined in from its own desires is able, at the same time, to let go; knowing that a wholesomely fulfilled relationship needs nothing more to return endlessly, without specific paths.

**Simply let emotions and thoughts flow by...**

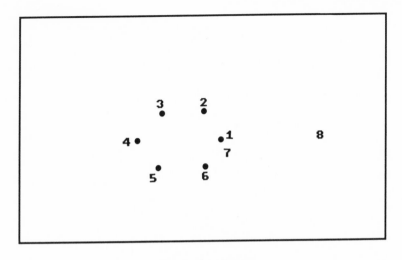

*Know, then let go*

In mindfulness, the past becomes less important, as does the future, because we see that, for example, "this is why I felt greed or hatred" or any other feeling. Had circumstances been different, there would have been some other transient response of my mind to the moment.

**See the actions of the world against the background of a still mind. . .**

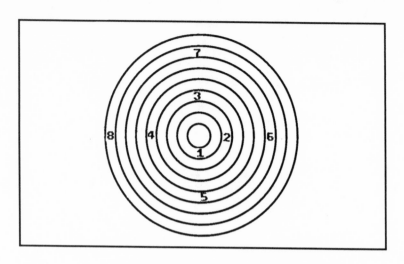

*Rooted in consciousness, attachment grows*

Each passing moment places us in new cycles of reality centered in transitiveness and insubstantiality. Unable to let go of each past reality, old growth rings imprison our senses, giving individuality to new objective forms. Unable to see clearly, we gather ever larger lines of defense against the vast emptiness beyond our senses, an emptiness awaiting to negate individual rings of experience. Successful sensory defenses against reality create a center which defines individual illusionary existence.

**With a still mind,
large actions of the world stand out more...**

*The little pool, sufficient to wet the feet, but too shallow for a bath*

Viewed as a bombardment of many arbitrary things on our mind, our attachment to the present is more apparent than real. In practical terms we participate in the world in a moderate, middle way, neither adorning the efforts of our mind nor chastising our body for existing.

**With a still mind,
small actions of the world become apparent. . .**

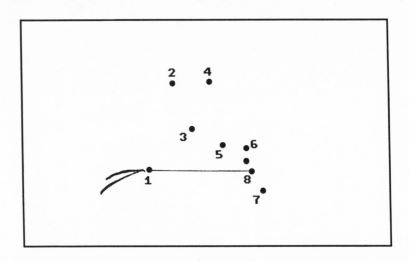

*Birds plane their wings upon the initial upsoaring*

To intuitively experience the nature of our own reality is extremely rare, because it is the nature of our ego to protect and preserve itself. Insight meditation is a technique for maintaining a parallelism between ego and consciousness; to adjust our minds, to see ourselves in the act of existing. At its core, intuitive experience needs no refinement.

**We accept the teachings of our mind. . .**

# FIND JOY IN WATCHFULNESS; GUARD WELL YOUR MIND

— *Endurance,* Dhammapada

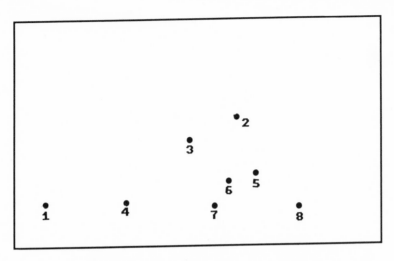

*The flood of joy, like breakers on a seashore*

This path's premise for calming the mind, through meditation, is that we are able to seriously focus on only one thing at a time. The one thing which appears again and again, endlessly, is breath at the gate of our nose. There is no need to search further for life's recurring waves.

**We are alone, not lonely. . .**

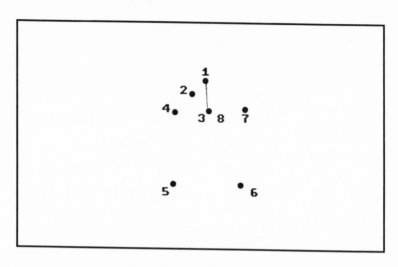

*Fire does not burn itself*

Being aware of our breath lets us become aware of our body, feelings, perceptions, motivations and memories. Aware of all these things burning within us, we can know the dependent origination in which we find our self at any moment. The flame of craving never consumes itself, but merely awaits a vanishing of the mind's fuel.

**May my mind be a mirror to confrontation. . .**

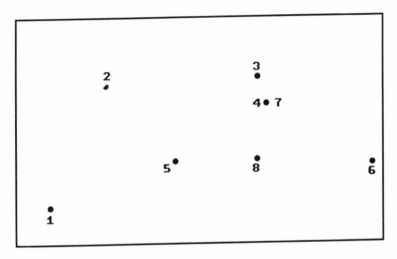

*Fishermen spread their nets over the river*

To follow a middle way, devoid of ego-driven extremes, is to reflect on threads of truth. A calm balanced mind serves as an excellent net, able to catch us from falling into superstition and prejudice. Threads of truth, from direct experience, have been woven together into a net stretched across the centuries, knotted with discourses and drawn tight with aphorisms.

**My mirror mind reflects all equally,
the pretty and the ugly...**

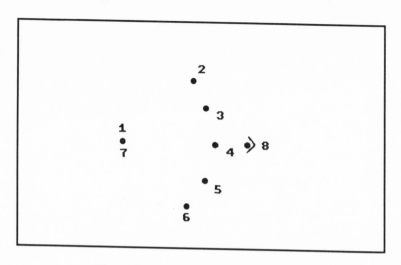

*The archer shoots with the whole bow*

Meditation's practice, then, may start by being aware of and focusing on breathing. The value is not so much what we are focused on, as it is what is blocked out; but it is a first step at moving outside our ego to observe, with all our concentration, at least one aspect of our existence. Catching glimpses of higher functioning comes with additional practice.

**My mirror mind doesn't retain. . .**

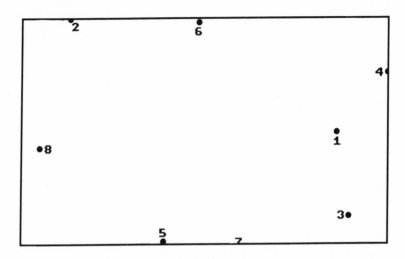

*Dependent upon these things, now flees*

Viewing suffering caused by craving, we sit. Viewing peace rising from craving's ashes, we know it is our judging mind which keeps us from being at one with the world as it really is. Wrapping our no-self in impermanence we can arise and enter freedom's path. As a coconut never breaks symmetrically, we know the way will be neither perfectly smooth nor totally harmful; it will simply be.

**My mirror mind doesn't judge. . .**

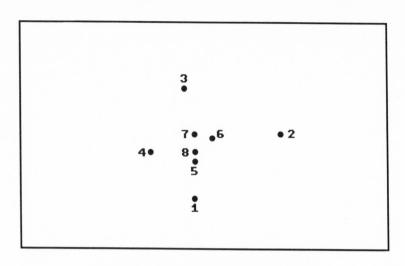

*Neither in the sky, nor deep in the ocean,*
*can we be free of our evil*

Snail shells and distant stars spiral to a same dark inner void. This path is a reflective paradox of looking out and seeing in. The impractical, apparently lying beyond our present reality, becomes of greatest utility while expedient shells fall away as ultimately worthless. Knowledge of the infinite subtleties of an insubstantial mind is a powerful tool. Together with the action of doing nothing, this knowledge can help resolve specific and immediate problems in our life. Watching from aside, we stand in the midst of conquering our own weakness.

**My mirror mind washes itself clean. . .**

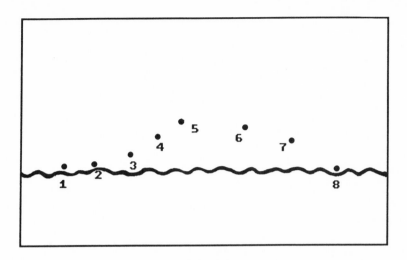

*Make an island for yourself*

This path is based on personal experience, a standing apart from the shifting whims which propel the wave of humanity all about us. Rational understanding stands above the cacophony of worldly declarations of gain or loss, praise or blame, fame or anonymity. To rise above a sea of suffering requires skilful mastery of a self which is impermanent and insubstantial. We lose our way by lashing our senses to the physical beings, feelings, perceptions, volitions and consciousness of others.

**All sounds are the same. . .**

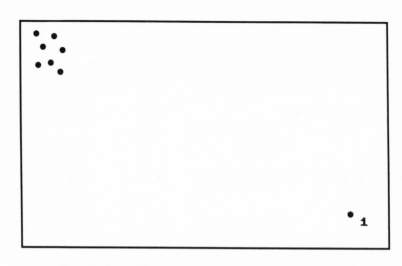

*Travel alone, like a great elephant alone in the forest*

Mindful of our inner impulses, of each momentary action, and life's transitiveness, we continue on alone. Calm and insightful, we near the no-end of our path.

**Just listen. . .**

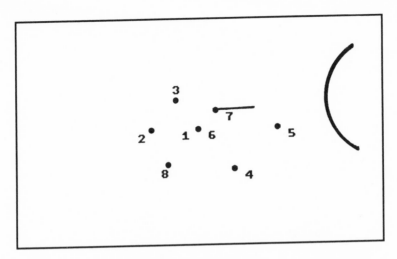

*Mosquitos have no inducement to alight on a hot iron ball*

At the completion of this meditation, worldly dependencies once again pour in, uninvited, upon us; but with reduced intensity and effect. Approaching our goal, we remain alert and aware of all about us, yet not deluded that our state of mind is an ultimate reality.

**Labels in our minds cause us to judge the sounds. . .**

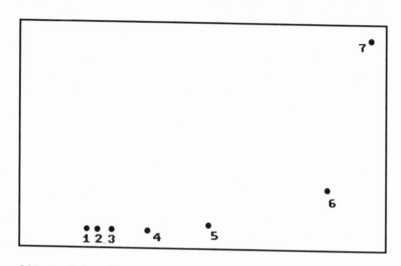

*Objects of thought are infinite if the heart embraces large numbers*

In its essence, consciousness is similar for all sentient beings. Therefore, we would do nothing to harm any other
consciousness, for we are all of the same fabric. In this
way, the heart can embrace more than the mind can know.

**Judging sounds sets off a chain of thought. . .**

# OUR LIFE
# IS THE CREATION OF OUR MIND

— *Contrary Ways*, Dhammapada

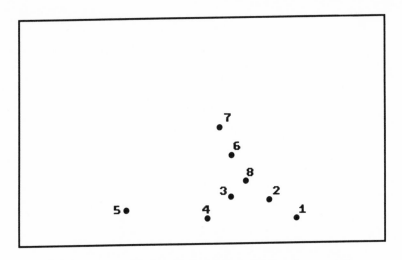

*All senses, save touch, are as cotton wool on four anvils,*
*deadening the hammer's blow*

It is the static subject/object dichotomy maintained by
ego's hold on I/not I, which permits a perception of other
beings, events and phenomena as somehow unrelated or
hostile to us. To know that what we fear is ourselves, is to
strip away false defenses.

**A chain of thought sets off a chain of emotions. . .**

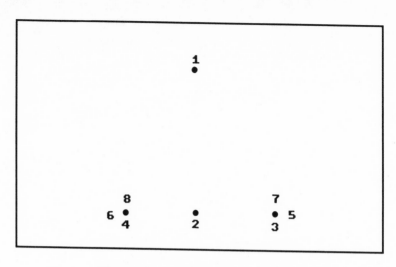

*The sea is not swollen by its streams*

We are thus called to overcome ourselves. Without illusion, we sit; acutely attending to sounds, thoughts and feelings. As streams are washed by grains of sand, impure traces are cast out by an expansive mind.

**Quiet my mind chatter. . .**

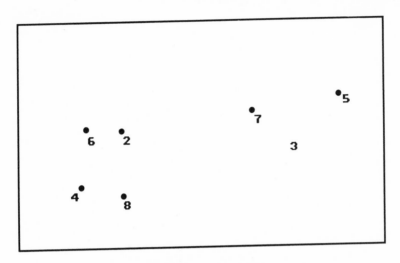

*No self here, no self there*

It is as important to know who we are not, as it is to know
who we are. Are we only our mind? Are we something
other than our mind? Do we own our mind? Is our mind
our only sovereign power? False beliefs about our identity
lead to false emotions. False emotions lead to false actions
in defense of an unreal self.

**Just sit. . .**

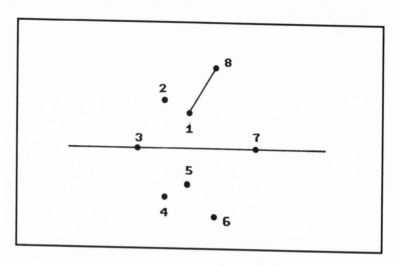

*A mountain and its reflection*

Mountain and valley, light and shadow, thought and action; they are all part of the same melody. This path is not an invitation to worldly retreat, but a charge to be alive, awake and aware.

**When I eat, I will be aware I eat. . .**

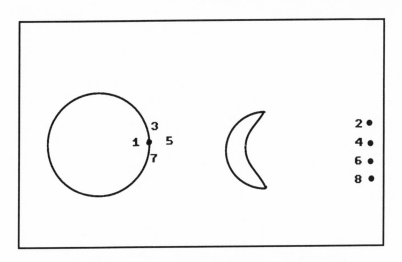

*The crescent moon is dimmed by the sun's splendor*

Having climbed to a clear view of wholesomeness, we must take care not to fall. As flowers turn to the sun, we need to turn our mind toward the present arising now and turn away from shadows of the past.

**When I wash, I will be aware I wash. . .**

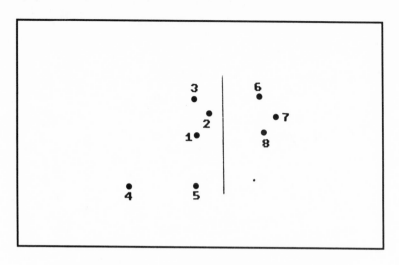

*The force of the way is to live through, not just to*

At times we must yield, turning our mind away from evil, thereby weakening its hold on us. We then can turn again, keeping our mind clear to see new traces of evil arising. By facing away from any promised semblance of evil's temporary pleasure, we can nurture views opposite to it. To understand impermanence is to understand the potential for weakening the grip of evil on our mind.

**When I read, I will be aware I read. . .**

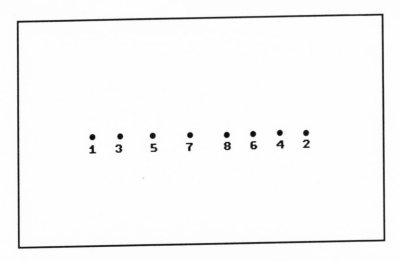

*Accepting our small self for what it is not,*
*is to know what our big self is*

Being free of attachments in our mind, our emptiness is filled with a sense of a true self, with a sense of making room for others in our life, with a sense of being able to react authentically to the moment with our entire being.

**When I breathe, I will be aware I breathe. . .**

# SELF IS LORD OF SELF

— *Self*, Dhammapada

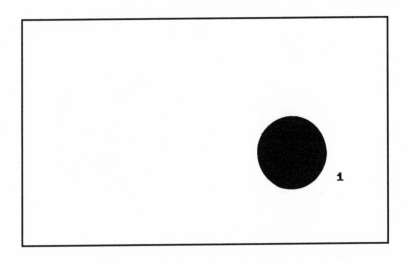

*The stupefied and homogeneous ego lacks its own nature*

This path focuses on one central question; apart from a self swollen by attachment, who are we? This path's answer is that our true nature can neither be touched nor described. Rather it is a continuous process, a movement away from greed, hatred and delusion.

**May myself be well and happy...**

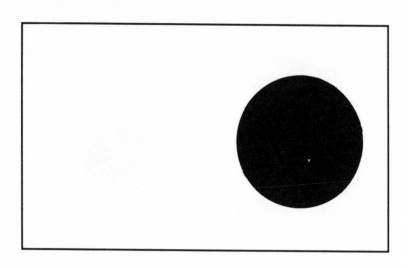

*What is the true self entailed in a separation from the reference systems?*

This path points the way to the beginning of an end, the ending of an unwholesome mind. With its passing, a nothingness, which is unconnected and without reference, grows within us; thus, we are fulfilled because of our emptiness.

**May a loved one be well and happy. . .**

*The true self is non-life, an absolute negative;*
*a dropping off of mind and body*

This path's end comes with a complete parting of the ways.
It is a saying of goodbye to unwholesome attachments.

**May one I dislike be well and happy. . .**

*The true self is life, an absolute affirmative;*
*the mind and body dropped off*

At the very moment we become aware of the void in our existence, we can become aware of our true nature. We can wake up to the beginning of a speck of light shining on our own reality, which, in fact, originates from this same empty self.

**May all living creatures be well and happy. . .**

*Non-life turns into life, not one, not different. . .*
*a single beautiful gem*

Becoming nothing and being nothing form endless links in
the same chain of existence. Sand and rock, right and
wrong, cloud and sea, life and death become but definitions of one another.

**Just sit. . .**

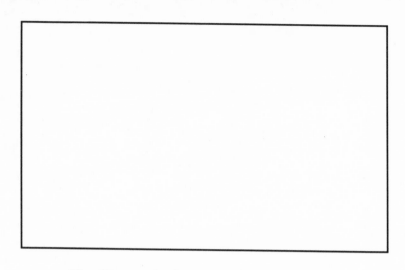

*Non-life, non-death, no increase, no decrease. . .*
*the world of nirvana*

This path, just taken, teaches that our existence is a continuous meeting of endings and beginnings. We are able to join these meetings, to be at one with our true nature, only at each changing moment, in the void of the enlightened now.

**Just breathe. . .**

# SOURCES

*Psychological Studies on Zen*, Yoshiharu Akishige, Maruzen Co. Ltd., Tokyo, 1977.

*Buddhist Psychology*, Caroline A. F. Rhys Davids, Oriental Books, Reprint Corporation, 54 Rani Thansi Road, New Dehli-55, 1975.

*Buddhist Psychology*, 2nd edition, Padmasiri de Silva, McMillan Academic and Professional Ltd., London, 1991.

*The Psychology and Philosophy of Buddhism*, W. F. Jayasuriya, Buddhist Missionary Society, Brickfields, Kuala Lumpur 0-9-06, Malaysia, 1988.

*Buddhist Meditation and Depth Psychology*, R. Burns, Buddhist Publication Society, Kandy, Sri Lanka, 1981.

*Freudian and Buddhist Psychology*, Padmasiri de Silva, Lake House Investments Ltd., Colombo 2, Sri Lanka, 1978.

*Religion and Nothingness*, Keji Nishitani, University of California Press, 1982.

*The Dhammapada*, Juan Masaro, Viking Penquin Inc., 1988.

*The Wisdom of China and India*, Lin Yutang, The Modern Library, 1955.

*Zen Mind, Beginner's Mind*, Shumya Suzuki, Weatherhill, 1990.

*Tao Te Ching*, Gia-Fu Feng and Jane English, Vintage Books, 1974.

*A Manual of Abhidhamma*, Narada Maha Thera, Buddhist Publication Society, Kandy, Sri Lanka, 1968.

*One Foot In The World*, Lilly de Silva, Buddhist Publication Society, Kandy, Sri Lanka, 1986.

*The Teachings of the Compassionate Buddha*, E. A. Burtt, New American Library, 1982.

*A Taste of Freedom*, Ven. Ajahn Chah, Buddhist Publication Society, Kandy, Sri Lanka, 1988.

*Zen Buddhism and Psychoanalysis*, D. T. Suzuki, et.al., Harper, 1970.

*Zen Keys*, Thich Nhat Hanh, Anchor Books, 1974.

*The Field of Zen*, D.T. Suzuki, Perennial Library, 1969.

*Essays in Zen Buddhism*, D.T. Suzuki, Grove Press, 1961.

*A Western Approach to Zen*, C. Humphreys, Quest Book, 1971.

*Buddhist Meditation*, Piyadassi Thera, Buddhist Publication Society, 1978.

*A Manual of Buddhism*, Narada Thera, Buddhist Missionary Society, 1971.

*Pali Buddhist Texts*, R.E.A.Johansson, Curzon Press, 1983.

*The Heart of Buddhist Meditation*, Nyanaponika Thera, Rider, 1983.

*Fundamentals of Buddhist Ethics*, Gunapala Dharmasiri, Buddhist Research Society, 1986.